Glass Roses
Prose & Poetry

A N E

Dedication:
To everyone who thought they were a lot to handle,
Everyone who felt they weren't enough,
Everyone who felt like they were an imposter
in their own life:
I see you.
We are not the same but you will never be alone.
We are roses on the same bush, growing in different
directions.

To my younger self,
I wish I could go back & tell you it gets better.

Glass Roses: Prose & Poetry
by A N E

ISBN: 979-8-9879115-1-8

This Book Contains Elements of:

Sexual Assault
Depression/Anxiety
PTSD
Suicide
Abandonment
Losing friends/family
Love & Heartache

Table of Contents

Finding Ways to Learn a New Language
I'll Walk With You Once Upon a Dream
Traumatic Memories
No Matter How Many Shower I Take, It Won't Go Away
Anxiety: a Nightmare
Social Anxiety
When Oversenory Meets a Noisy World
Maybe I Was Never Meant to Fit In
We All Have Our Addictions
In My Quiet
The Haunting
Unforgivable Pasts
Suicide Attempts
The Shadows of Reputation
Give Me a Reasons to Change My Mind
No, You Don't Get a Proper Goodbye
Depression is My Isolation
To Blow a Candle Out or Watch it Burn
Lower Them Down
Out Running Shadows
Friends Wouldn't Be The Right Word
My Greatest Enemy is Myself
Why Can't I Be Perfect?
To Be a Healer
To Be An Empath
Feeling Post-Apocalyptic
Regret Will Swallow Me Whole

Stories aren't always as they appear,
we are bent & shaped
a certain way,
it bleeds into the way we breathe
this very air.
Don't let anyone tell you
that your story doesn't belong
in this world of ours.

What if I told you
society trains us to be quiet
to keep safe
this utopia they made up.

Utopia isn't real
if the truth lies
behind muffled sounds &
closed doors.

Speak louder
until they stop & hear you,
reach out for empathy
until they see you.
Truth is not known
until every side speaks.

So let us speak.
Our voices, though shaking,

will move mountains &
shape the earth,
for we've become united.

-Together-

We were raised
to be silent
about things that matter.
We were taught
to turn a blind eye
at conflict all around us.
A world of chaos
where screams are muted &
surprise is feigned
at how people are treated.

When did we become comfortable
only defending our own?
When did the suffering
of those around us
become a mere inconvenience
to our days ahead?

Perhaps our world did die long ago.
for even the churches lack empathy &
hospitals are no longer concerned
about the sick & dying.

Can compassion be resuscitated?

-Hearts Dark as Coal-

She has always been so giving of herself,
going above & beyond
to make everyone around her feel cared for.
If you ask for an hour of her time,
she'd give you a day;
If you needed help,
she'd be there every step of the way.
She pours a part of herself
into everything she does
without hesitation,
because she knows how it feels
to be unwanted or alone &
she never wants to be the reason
someone else feels the way she does.
She'll burn herself out
for a world who wouldn't look twice
in her direction.

-The Saddest Girls Are Often The Kindest-

She can talk a lot
but often says so little
with the words she uses.
Small talk
is a requirement,
knowing her heart
is a privilege.

-Her Inner Circle; Ode to an ENFJ-

Your opinions of her
are your own.
They do not belong to her &,
though they can hurt her,
they do not define
who she really is &
will not stop her
from becoming
who she is meant to be.

-She Defined Herself, Not You-

Don't be afraid to soar, darling,
you were never meant
to stay on the ground.
God gave you wings
so you can get your feet
off the ground &
see the world in a whole new way.
Don't let fear stop you
from learning how to fly.

-Like Icarus, You're Made to Touch The Sun-

She was like rain
on a sunny day,
spreading colors across the sky
creating her own kind of rainbow.
She was the kind of storm
you never get enough of,
she was the rain
you danced with,
not caring who was watching.

-She Was Rain Itself-

On days where anxiety is loud,
let me know
so I can speak love louder.
I will sit with you,
keeping you company
on days where love
cannot be heard
more than a whisper.

-Can I Keep You Company in The Shadows?-

Underneath all the pain,
the trauma,
self-hatred, &
anger
was a compassionate healer
waiting to resurface.
Her touch was soft
as she comforted those in pain,
her words were gentle
as if they were meant to
pick up the broken pieces
of every person she spoke to.

-Empathy Was Her Super Power-

She was always my spark of hope
in darker hours
reminding me that I am loved,
that we are brave.
She doesn't point out
how much longer we have left to go,
only how far we've come &
how much we've grown.
I have this theory
that God gave me
a guardian angel in human form,
she's far too kind for this world.
Thinking she deserves so much less
then she is to others,
she doesn't put herself first
as often as she should
but she knows how to stand up
for those around her
with no hesitation.
I just wish she'd realize
she deserves the best too.

-My Guardian Angel-

She had dark blue eyes,
the color of a raging sea,
trapped inside the smallest drop of water.
A storm
waiting to be set free.

-Don't Push Her-

She pressed forward,
not letting the world
tame the fire
inside of her soul.

-Persistence-

She was like a rose
in the middle of the desert,
growing all on her own,
even in the hardest circumstances
becoming something so beautiful.

-Desert Rose-

Twenty-six letters in the alphabet.
There was once a time
where she would use them in variety,
as a knife,
cutting herself down to the level
she thought she deserved.
She's grown so much since then,
now using her words like a sword
standing up for those who can't &
defending what is right.
Her heart,
though scarred & bruised,
is stronger than it was before.
She chooses her battles wisely
knowing God will be by her side,
she knows
that even on her darkest days
she is not alone.

-She Found Ways to Nurture Her Inner Voice-

Don't stress over what you don't have.
Darling,
your imperfections
are what make you perfect
to me.

-In The Eye of The Beholder-

What a beautiful soul I see in you,
made up of so many fascinating things
that paints a lovely picture
in my head.
Your teasing & sarcasm are soaked in the words,
"I really do care."
You wear concern on your face, &
family holds do much more meaning to you
than it ever has for me.
You interest me.
Around you,
I have no obligation to be anyone
other than myself.
You made me feel so important,
if only for a little while.
Long after I forget your face,
I'll still remember
the kind of friend you were to me.

-Heart on Your Sleeve-

Seeking a place to belong &
someone to love her,
she reached out to those around her
breaking the dark habits
that had become her very nature.
This was the beginning of something new,
something better
than she had been used to.

-Pull Her Toward Healing-

She had grown her own flowers
for the world would not
spare her any;
She hid them away
out of fear
of her garden being taken away.

-Flowers of Kindness-

You were an intense kind of personality.
A shot of whiskey
at a wine tasting,
an extra sweet tea
on a hot northern day.
You weren't everyone's favorite thing
but that's okay,
the right people
will love you the same.

-You Will Find Your Tribe-

She was the most fascinating
kind of girl,
mending her broken pieces &
finding parts of who she was
inside all the books she read.
Every book she's ever held
has touched her soul,
never leaving her the same
as she was before.
She did not rely
on those around her
to fix her heart,
for they were the ones
who broke it in the first place.
This is why she believes
God gave her books,
she could rely on them
to show her all the things
this world could not.

-The Glass Reader-

There is a scared girl,
unprepared & told
she has no other options.
Tears run down her face,
her parents telling her she's too young,
she has too much to live for to let this ruin her.

A single woman
who was left when the news broke out,
she was old enough to know
that she couldn't do this on her own.
Searching for help so maybe they could both live
but turned away by those
who were meant to care most.

Shaking in fear as she holds the test results,
a rape victim terrified of her own body.
She doesn't want anyone to know,
she had already been told
that the way he touched her body had been her fault.
the clothes she wore
any words she could've said
being out alone
not having a way to protect herself
just breathing this very air.
She had done nothing wrong
but believed everyone's words
when they told her that she could've prevented it.

The ones that made her feel like
what was growing in her body
was an abomination, just like her.

If we loved them as we should,
if we reached out &
offered the help
they had once asked for with compassion &
the support they so desperately needed
it could've changed the world.

-Those We Condemned in Hatred-

The way he touched your body
does not take away
from your worth.
Those things he told you
about yourself,
the way he made you feel,
speak volumes of his soul
not yours.
Running fingers across your skin
he whispers that you want it,
you never did
but you still find yourself
defending his actions.
The hardest part
is fully admitting to yourself
that he was your abuser.
That is where your healing begins.

-Though Domestic, it's Still Abuse-

The pain &
the hurt;
All the things
that chipped away
at our souls,
broke our hearts, &
shattered our lives;
As we turned to healing,
those pieces are stitched together
in different ways than before.
Using silver & gold in the seam work,
God is creating something new in you.
Let yourself heal, darling,
sad days may come
don't let those dull your smile &
stop your dancing.
You are a work of art
in motion.

-Kintsugi: The Art to Repair With Gold-

Sometimes in this world
things are never quite
what they seem.
People aren't who they appear
on the surface,
be careful with the words you say
for you don't know the day
they're going through.
You don't know every detail
of their past
to understand why they made a choice
you disagree with.
We are called to love others &
help them grow in love;
picking one side or another
in this judgmental world
is like building a wall &
choosing only to love those on your side.
Love your enemies too.

-A Little Kindness Goes A Long Way-

Everyone is who they are
no matter what is thought of them,
their choices made
are a result of where they've been &
what had been done to them.
They may not line up with
how you would see things
but in time spent getting to know
the souls you're so ready to condemn,
you can find a different outcome.

-Everyone's Story is Worth Listening to-

Politeness is one of my greatest enemies,
as I see people all over the world
walk over eggshells &
into uncertainty.
We've grown comfortable
in acts of indifference,
it's hard to tell those who love us
from those who are scared
to hurt our feelings.
Having wanted to leave for so long,
we've settled for mediocre people
who barely tolerate us
because we fear being alone.
What if I told you
that the loneliness fades
as the earth keeps spinning &
you'll find people
worthy of your time.
Just be patient
understand your worth
as you do the worth
of those around you too.
Let honesty, over fear,
lead your life &
through this
may the world be changed.

-Broken Societal Norms-

A princess unaware of her worth,
a price unexplainable of the crown
that sits upon her head,
listens to the words of an enemy
disguised as a teacher.
They tell her that she is responsible
for all that is done unto her,
for every man who touches her against her will,
for every tear she couldn't help but cry,
for the blood that covers her skin
once he walks away.
The words she had been brought up with
tell her that her body
is merely a stop
for men passing by.
She believed she was no one to be cherished
but a vessel for someone else's pleasure
through her screams of pain,
love wasn't supposed to feel like this
was this love?
He tells her yes,
that she should be grateful
someone wants her at all.
If only someone would show her,
her value is far beyond diamonds & gold,
that no one could take it away from her.

-She Was Priceless-

They think I'm paranoid
when I jump at someone's touch,
they don't know my past.

The rude comments I hear
when someone steps towards me
for a hug &
I step away,
they don't know why I'm scared.

I've been laughed at & teased
for shuttering at the thought
of physical intimacy,
but they don't know me.

They don't know you.
They've never heard
the details of that story,
they never will.

I'd rather hear their judgments & cruelties,
than being lectured on how I could've prevented this.
I couldn't. Nothing will change that.

-No Matter What They Think of Me-

You used your apologies
to manipulate me into staying,
I was a monster
if I walked away from someone in need.

"I'm still trying to change."

"I'll get better, just give me more time."

You used me for far too long
with no intentions of ever changing,
you were too comfortable
in who you were.
The smartest manipulator I know,
you admitted everything you did to me &
made me feel like your saving grace,
the reason you'd leave your past behind.

You'd tell me how much you needed me &
I fell for it every time.
I was your enabler for far too long,
your apologies have become wasted air
until you finally choose to change.

-I Hope You Change For The Next Girl-

His hands on my shaking body,
skin against skin,
I kept saying no
asking him to stop
but the sound of my voice
became nothingness.
I felt like a stranger
on the sidelines
as I watched everything
being taken away from me.

-Trauma in 3rd Person-

His hands were in places
they never belonged,
you wanted him to stop
he's no longer listening.
Your cries are replaced with silence
after a while,
afraid you'll anger him
if you try to get away.
He's gone now
but the feeling stays,
you're still scared
of those offering
the most innocent of touches.

-I Never Called it Rape-

You weren't a monster in the beginning.
You never laid it on all at once,
that's what people don't get,
it wasn't until I was looking back
that I saw all the damaged you had done.
When I first knew you
it was innocent touches
while we laughed at horrible puns,
it was sharing the same taste in music &
knowing that someone else was willing
to listen to sad songs with me.
You made me feel like a choice
even when no one else was picking me.
The thing is
you never chose me either,
you just let me choose you
over & over again.

-Is it Possible to Miss You as a Friend?-

When I told someone for the first time
I made you out to be a stranger,
was that for me or you?
I don't know.
Maybe in some way
after what you did,
I still wanted to protect you.
It didn't make me love you less
like people said it should,
I felt disgusted & unloved
by the one I loved most.
It was trust
that was broken.

-Or Was It Me?-

You scream at me
as I try to tell you
what had been done to me.
How hard it was
to even get these words out &
you acted like it was my fault,
scolding me for my actions &
how they didn't line up
with what you thought was right.
You back me into a corner with your words,
making my nothingness feel even less.
"Maybe it wasn't rape,"
the words slip from my mouth
before I could pull them back.
I didn't like lying to you
but at least you stopped yelling.
You were the one
who taught me to be silent,
because if you couldn't handle it.
Who could?

**-I Took My Voice Back, it Wasn't Yours to Keep
Anyways-**

I wasn't your normal girl growing up,
I was a bully for a short time,
I was dark & cold,
trying to convince myself
that I did not need
nor did I deserve kindness.
I did not want to be pitied
so my mind went to be feared,
ah yes,
I'd rather be feared than pitied
any day of my life.
I wanted to belong
to find a community
accepting of me,
marriage wasn't a desire
yet when seeking comfort
I often looked in the arms
of men who promised me the world
so they could use me.
I didn't want what they promised,
I just wanted to make the loneliness melt away &
it never did.
They shattered my pieces a little more,
leaving a void that felt unfillable.
Are they really monsters
if I was using them too?

-What if We Were All Monsters?-

I will never again take for granted
the power of a hot shower
on a sad morning.
I'll never stop appreciating
the ability to stand there
as water washes away
all my depressive thoughts,
all my nightmares from the night before.
You never know what you have
until it's gone,
until your legs are too weak
to hold your body up,
until it hurts too much
to stand in the water.

-When Sickness Takes The Best of Me-

I am stuck in my head.
Sometimes I feel like the real me
is looking through a window
banging on glass
screaming to get out.
I am not heard.
I have no control.
I am,
I exist,
I breathe a certain way
that makes me different from others.
When will I stop being a prisoner
of my own mind?
Mental illness
is my prison guard,
I was born with chains &
I'll wear them until the day I die.

-When Will I be Set Free?-

I wish I knew now to tell you
what my anxiety is doing to me.
I wish I could explain
what I needed &
have you understand
that this isn't me,
the real me is trapped inside;
But I can't,
it won't let me.
Anxiety has sown my mouth shut,
it tells me you don't want me around,
it says you're only with me
because nothing better came along.
Sitting with a group of friends,
anxiety would whisper in my ear
that I was bringing the mood down,
if I weren't there then they'd have fun.
I need you to tell me it's wrong,
I need you to say that you want me around,
that you're with me because of me.
Words aren't a love language of my soul,
they're a peace of mind
for the storm inside my head.
I wish I didn't need them as much as I do.

-Maybe My Anxiety Was Right-

We are only as alone
as we let ourselves be.
Just remember,
in those dark moments
when worry outweighs
our desperate need for connection,
taking moments of solitude &
pushing the world away
are two very different things.

-The World Hasn't Turned its Back on Us Yet-

It's a little colder than I expected
feeling like ice inside my chest,
when indifference is met
with the loneliness I hold close
in this life.
It's eating me alive,
yet, parting ways with it
feels like saying goodbye
to the one constant friend I've had.
Maybe I choose this for myself
because, to be whole & wholly loved
is foreign to me.
An unknown future like that
is what terrifies me.

-Healing Feels Like Losing a Part of Me-

Blood ran down my thighs
covering my soft skin
in a crimson color,
I found release in the way
I drew pictures
with this knife.
The deluge of emotion
faded slowly
as I got lost
in the color spilling.
I grew & healed
as time passed,
finding that my art
didn't have to hurt
like it once did.
Knives replaced
with markers & pens,
my body still a canvas
to be covered.
Emotions still expressed
in the way color glides
across my skin
in a whole new way.

-My Releases Ever-Changing-

I lay down,
not because I'm tired,
I long for an escape
in my dreams
when I no longer
want to be in this world.

-Naps-

I'm not autistic enough for you,
though I don't pick up on your passive hints
or subtext in our conversation.
You get mad at me.

I'm not autistic enough for you,
while you're embarrassed of me &
how I can't read social cues
or public situations.
You tell me I could do better.

I'm not autistic enough for you,
while we argue
over the feelings I didn't see you having
& how I should've known
what you never told me.

I'm not autistic enough,
while I have a meltdown at Walmart
in the condiment aisle
because I forgot my headphones
& pushed myself to go in anyway;
You tell me to get off the floor,
I'm making a fool of myself.

I'm not autistic enough for you
while I'm sitting in a dark room
rocking back & forth, crying,

because my routine was disrupted
one too many times today.
You tell me to get over it,
this is how the real world works.

I'm not autistic enough for you
because you don't want me
to be disabled.
What you don't understand is
I'm still autistic no matter
who doesn't think I should be.

-"Are You Sure You're Autistic?"-

I am suicidal today.
It doesn't look the way
you think it should.
I'm not creeping in a dark room
covered in blood
cursing the world
For doing me wrong.
The world didn't do anything to me.
Instead,
I ask you how your day is &
listen sincerely for your every thought;
I say *I love you* often &
with more depth than I ever have before.
I know I seem absent-minded,
I'm stuck in my head more today.
The laugh I share today doesn't seem fake &
I force genuine smiles
as if those whisper my silent goodbyes.
I hold doors open for strangers & tell them
I hope you have a good day,
I genuinely hope your day is going better than mine.
I am suicidal today,
my depression has gotten the best of me &
I want to end it all,
I'm yearning for someone
to talk me out of it.

I told you I felt more depressed days ago &
I needed to talk things out,
You were busy then.
You're still busy now.
Everyone's busy.
There's no one to say goodbye to,
maybe I will die alone.

-A Suicide Note-

As children we are shown
how to play games of pretend,
games of stoneface-
not letting another person
affect your outward expression;
Games of house
or work
or school.
How quick we were to want to grow up,
now that I'm older
I realized we never stopped playing
these games.

We pretend to be okay,
when we want to cry,
scream,
be anywhere but where we are.

We pretend to be whole,
while we carry shattered pieces inside
that tear us apart.
Our brokenness is killing us,
while we pretend it's nothing at all.

We pretend to be unphased
by the words said to us,
trying our best
to not let our faces betray us.

We pretend to be these perfect people
that the world expects us to be.
What our religious group,
our social circles, &
our society wants us to be.

I made myself fit in this mold,
I scoffed at those
who weren't as good at pretending as me.

I was so good at what I did,
I convinced myself
that I wasn't pretending at all.

This is the problem I see.

We. Are. Not. Perfect.
Nor should we be expected to act as if we were.

We are loved for our imperfections
by a perfect God.

We live in mercy
under grace,
not because we held our heads high &
pretended we were something we're not.

We are all made up of broken pieces,
heartache, &
tears.

We make mistakes,
we hurt people,
we mess up,
we're wrong sometimes...
or most of the time.
Pretending problems don't exist
won't make them any less real
in your life.

You are you.
Keep growing,
keep changing,
be who you are
because God wants you for you,
not who you pretended to be.

-We Never Stop Playing-

My body is falling apart,
it's driving me insane.
I keep pushing myself anyways
in trying to get better
for it's the little things
that I miss the most
about a healthy life.

-Withering Away-

Hospital gowns are far too familiar,
the doctors all seem to know me by name.
Test after test
you'd think they would've fixed me by now,
or maybe just put a label
on what's wrong.
Yet, here I am,
still the same,
just as sick as day one.

We're all dying slowly
in this present world,
my death may arrive
a little sooner than the rest is all.
Though I don't know when,
I feel it in my gut,
I know it'll be soon &,
though it terrifies me,
I'll be ready for it when it comes.

-Maybe They'll Have Better Luck Helping The Next Person-

What you told me
to just get over
is not a curable disease,
there's no going away soon or
growing out of it.
It lurks in the shadows around me
waiting to pounce
at the most inconvenient times.
Don't tell me it's not real,
I know it's not real.
I know it's all in my head.
Do you think I want to replay
the most traumatic day of my life
over & over again
without even closing my eyes?
No.
Don't tell me I'm just being dramatic,
if you were describing horrifying scenes
on a seemingly normal day,
people would think you're being dramatic too.

-Post Traumatic Stress Disorder-

My nightmares are
written in a language
I do not understand,
bringing a miscommunication
between my mind & body.
They're a whole new world
to be explored,
a storybook
opened to the first page
for me to read
if only I take them
one step at a time.

-Finding Ways to Learn a New Language-

Though we may not have met yet,
I wish to feel your arms
wrapped around me,
as I cry on my bed;
Not because I am weak,
because we are stronger together.
I want your hand to hold
when my pain becomes too much &
I need someone to be my anchor.
I'd like to know what it's like
to wake up after a nightmare &
hear your calming voice
reminding me that everything will be okay,
as if you hadn't been woken up
by my countless screams.
To know that you see my broken pieces &
have decided I'm worth it all anyways.
To know that I am capable
of being loved.

-I'll Walk With You Once Upon a Dream-

Pictures of faces,
flashes of scenes,
a burst of light
every time I close my eyes.
There is a shaking in my bones,
my mind is scarred
beyond repair.

-Traumatic Memories-

Darkness stains my heart still
from the memory
of all that happened,
the pain still fresh
inside my mind.
I still have nightmares,
I thought they'd go away,
why haven't they gone away?
My body still shaking scared
when I wake up,
tears running down my cheeks,
I ask myself
how I could ever put someone through this.
How can I expect anyone to love
someone as broken as me?
No one deserves that kind of punishment.

**-No Matter How Many Showers I Take, it Won't Go
Away-**

With blood dripping from silver eyes
she watches me
through the white hairs
that hang in front of her face,
like a lion watching their prey.
Darkness surrounds her small figure
as she growls at my other nightmares,
they're scared of her too.
She's consumed so many souls
in this lifetime alone,
now it's my turn to go.

-Anxiety: A Nightmare-

I wasn't made the same as you,
stop telling me
how easy it's supposed to be.
You make friends everywhere you go.
Every room we walk into
someone knows your name,
this has always been easy for you.
All the while
I'm still stuck in my head
I'm trapped in a box,
not knowing
how to get out.

-Social Anxiety-

Like a one-sided window
I see everyone around me
but they don't see me.
I am trapped in my mind
with no way out.
I scream,
I shout,
you can't hear me.
To you, I am mute.
Tell me again
that I'm normal,
that nothing's wrong with me
when I'm a prisoner
of my own mind.
Tell me how to fix it,
tell me how to make it leave,
tell me how to stop my mind
from dragging me away
from the outside world too soon.
Tell me, please,
that on the days
where you can't hear me cry
inside my mind,
when I can't speak a single word
that you'll still sit by my side &
love me just the same.

-When Oversenory Meets a Complicated World-

I was the odd man out,
I was on the outside
of social cues &
happiness,
looking in
but unable to fit in.
I never did anything halfway,
if I talked
you could hear me
across the room &
in my silence
I could be mute for days.
I was never into the word "*like*",
why waste your time
with something that you're only
passively interested in?
When I was interested in anything,
I went all the way,
I was obsessive in my research &
poured hours of my time
into pursuing whatever my heart longed for.
The one thing that research could not teach me
was how to make a friend
or belong in the way
I've always wanted to.

-Maybe I Was Never Meant to Fit in-

I'm a broken introvert,
with a deep addiction
to socialization.
Such a dangerous drug
for me to mess with,
once I start down this path
it becomes harder for me
to recognize my need to be alone.
My craving for silence
is replaced with a fear
of being alone.
My words become empty,
meaningless,
only there to fill the void
I feel trapped in.
This addiction chips away
at my soul
until I don't even recognize myself.
It will come to a point
where I am so drained of energy
that it's physically painful
to be in a room with another soul;
Reminding me yet again,
why I was made the way I am.

-We All Have Our Addictions-

When words are no longer
on my side,
when I open my mouth
only to find
my voice has run away,
I will play you music.
Song after song,
pointing out words & phrases
that I cannot say
hoping that seeing me this way
teaches you I am loudest
in my silence &
that is when I need love
the most.

-In My Quiet-

No matter how far I run
this shadow still follows
behind me.
I can't escape my past
or those lies
you so easily believed about me.
Why can't you just leave me be?
Why can't you let me be happy?
You don't know the real me,
you only know
what you wanted to believe.
If only you understood
what I've been through &
what my darkness
has shaped me into.

-The Haunting-

My past is a noose
around my neck &
this is when I decide
if I let myself hang.
Memories become haunting echoes,
words once whispered
in endearing ways
are now reminders
that I can't go back & fix things.
Tug a little tighter & see how it feels
to be the one hurt & forgotten,
don't forget the feeling
if you live past this
you'll need it again someday.

-Unforgivable Pasts-

These words are written in blood.
There are so many
around that I've hurt,
so many lives I've destroyed.
My mind is a graveyard,
I've found no way out,
I killed myself
a thousand times
for the wrongs I've done.

-Suicide Attempts-

I get so angry
over people's opinions of me
because, in my mind,
I feel every bit deserving
of their negative thoughts
towards me.
I'm not mad at them
for saying I'm a monster,
I'm mad at myself
for being the monster
they hate so much.
I'm striving for healing,
I long for change,
but it's never enough.
I
am
not
enough.

-The Shadows of Reputation-

People move on.
Everyone moves on, &
when you walk away
like all those before you
I will be left with
nothing more
than broken promises &
a lonely heart.
When you tell me
you're different
I trust you a little less
in my heart.
Don't tell me you're different,
show me.

-Give Me a Reason to Change My Mind-

The hardest part
wasn't moving past
what had been done to me,
though that took years,
it was letting go of the bitterness
I had against all of you
who told me
I wasn't worth being loved anymore.
I hated you for so long,
cursing you all
for treating me like I was nothing.
Daily, I feel God whisper to me
'hate isn't worth it,'
it does nothing to you
but it holds me back.
So with these words,
I'm done.
I'm letting go
of you,
my hate,
my anger,
my bitterness.

I'm letting it all go & starting over.

-No, You Don't Get a Proper Goodbye-

I always try to hold close & comfort
those who are brokenhearted.
Yet, when my heart breaks,
it breaks alone.
The sound of it echoing
in this empty room,
reminds me
that I have no one.

-Depression is My Isolation-

It's not that I hate myself
or that day,
it's something entirely different
masked the same way.
I hate needing a distraction;
I hate remembering that I'm forgotten,
maybe I always will be;
I hate the disappointment
that ties a bow around broken promises;
I'd like to pretend a little longer
that I could be important to someone &,
if I don't tell them,
then I'm not so sad that they didn't know.
I'd rather make loneliness my fault
than face the truth.

-To Blow The Candle Out or Watch it Burn-

I convinced myself
that words were dead,
it was my way of hiding
from all the hurtful things
that were said to me.
If words had no power
I had no pain to feel,
no tears to cry,
no loneliness in my heart.
I don't want the world
to think they've won,
I don't want you to think
you've got to me.
Maybe if I tell myself enough
I'll be immune to your words,
& they'll stop haunting me.

-Lower Them Down-

The world spins around
the sun once more &
I'm back to where I once was.
Darkness creeps over my shoulder,
hiding in my shadows &
following my every step
pulling me back
into those memories I try to forget.
I hate myself
for the past I allowed &
the person I was once.
I'm constantly punishing myself
by carrying it into my future.
There will come a time,
there will be a day,
when my darkness will grow tired &
acceptance fully sets in
knowing that nothing can ever change.
What was done once before
cannot be rewritten
but who I was
will not define who I am
anymore.

-Out Running Shadows-

If everyone cares
as much as they claim
when they talk me off
the edge of the bridge,
then why can none of them
stand to look my direction
in the day to day life
long enough to say "hello".

-'Friends' Wouldn't be The Right Word-

You think the words you say
can damage me?
Foolish of you to claim,
for you have yet to hear
the words I say to myself.
My inner voice
has torn me down
at the smallest mistakes made,
reminding me how little
I'm worth.

-My Greatest Enemy is Myself-

Some days I'm on top of the world,
others I feel that
no matter how hard I try
I'll never get better.
I know in my head
that I can't be perfect
but my heart takes it personally
when my imperfections
become too real to me.

-Why Can't I Be Perfect?-

We walk around this world
with purpose in our hearts &
a gentle fire in our souls.
A longing to heal the world around us,
we take the pain of those
who come across our paths,
bruising our hearts
so deeply
sometimes life itself is hard to bear.
We take our time to recharge
with the idea of doing it all again
because we know what it's like to feel your pain,
& we'd rather hold it ourselves
than watch you suffer anymore.
In the end,
it helps us know
that everything will be okay for you.

-To Be a Healer-

Lovely souls
aren't made from a life
of sheltered innocence.
They are born in brutal fire
& dark words.
They're created in that moment
when they choose to hold gentleness
in their hearts still,
knowing that it isn't weakness
but a silent strength.
it's carrying softness in your soul
after seeing unthinkable things
in this world,
it's being hated &
choosing to love anyways.

-To Be an Empath-

It's crazy how things can change;
How streets you so often walked
start to feel dark,
the strangers you see in the store
now fill you with fear,
you feel like all eyes are on you.
A world you once saw as black & white
has faded gray,
& you don't know how to live anymore.

-Feeling Post-Apocalyptic-

My words.
They're all I have,
the blood I bleed.
Someday,
unspoken,
they'll be the death of me.

-Regret Will Swallow Me Whole-

Sometimes I miss you &
all the good memories we had together.
Remember that time when...?
... Yeah, it feels like forever ago.
We were so young back then
but it wasn't that long ago,
it was only a few years.
As much as I wish I could block you out,
I will never stop caring about you
in the back of my mind.
That's why I can't sit to talk,
all these memories keep coming back &
I don't trust myself.
I don't trust you either.

-Sitting in a Biggby Cafe-

All she wanted was to be a priority,
he always felt he couldn't be enough.
She wanted commitment
but he didn't know how
to face a world unknown &
trust someone new.
She asked him to follow her &
leave his past behind.
Fear overwhelms a heart that is weak,
nowhere near happiness
because at least there
he knows he's safe.

-Love Was Too Dangerous of a Dance-

You used to know
every part of my life,
now we are simply strangers
holding the keys to each other's secrets.

-I'll Take Yours to The Grave-

I fell back
into the old habits
I never thought I'd see again.
I broke your heart
because I never took time
to heal mine first.
Why do I forget how to love,
forget how to trust,
forget how to care for everyone
including myself.
Time & time again
it plays out in my head,
I want to fix it all.
You can't love someone properly,
you won't outgrow your toxic behaviors
until you learn to take care of yourself first.

-Maybe I Was Broken Beyond Repair-

A milestone in my healing
away from you
is looking back at all my lists
that you had changed &
all the little notes you wrote me
on my darker days.
Remembering that
before you broke me
you had been my friend
for a time.
I will never forget that.

-Words on The Golf Window-

Remember when we tried
cheating the system?
Remember how we tried
to let ourselves down easy
with cheat days &
coffee dates,
we didn't think we belonged together
but loneliness was too much to bear.
Looking back,
I realized we were only fooling ourselves
& that's what messed us up the most.

-We Should've Left Well Enough Alone-

No one quite prepares you
for the aftermath of a breakup.
The pain & loneliness to follow,
the crying
even though you saw this coming
miles away.
You check your phone
for the third time in the last hour,
no text messages yet.
You feel ghosted
but what did you expect
when you agreed to just be friends.
Relationships are like addictions,
breakups are like cutting off
cold turkey.

-You Were My Addiction-

I just wanted you to be happy,
I wanted to be in your life too.
It took me far too long to realize
that it wasn't how our story would end,
you could either be happy
or you could have me.
I didn't blame you for choosing happiness,
it just makes me sad
that it couldn't be both.

-Happiness Has No Limits & You Will Touch The Stars-

How does someone live
after the one who holds &
cares for your heart
has no choice but to walk away?
I was not made for good-byes
or grade school crushes,
I was made for goodnights,
forehead kisses,
& everlasting love.

-Where Was My Happily Ever After?-

Every time I look at you
breathing gets a little harder.
Friends, we agreed,
was better than nothing at all.
How I longed for you
to hold me in your arms
one last time &
tell me that
everything will be okay.
To kiss me goodnight
just one last time.

-I Was Naive to Think You Were The One-

I was wrong
in the way I treated you,
the words that left my lips out of anger
held intent to destroy,
not in search of the truth or understanding.
Bloodshed surprised me as a result,
hadn't this been the road I had chosen?
I was finding out that
I could be toxic too,
everyone can.
All there is left to do
is reach out to make amends
with the souls you've hurt
while finding a better road
to walk in life.

-I Don't Blame You For Leaving Me-

Even when we've both grown older &
our hearts have chosen
different paths,
I hope to sit down beside you
with a cup of coffee in hand.
I hope we can still talk
as openly as we use to
with no fear of judgment or
harm in honest opinions.
If ever I have a friend like this,
I hope to be old & gray,
just to see that it's always been you.
To come from separate lives &
care enough to make them one,
that's what best friends are for.

-I'm Sorry This Couldn't Be Our Ending-

When I pushed you away
saying all I did was right,
the world dimmed down for me
blacker than the darkest night.
I turned back to you
begging you to forgive me,
you looked past me
through tear-stained eyes
as if I were a ghost you couldn't see.
That should've been my cue
to leave you be
but that was the moment
the hurt really settled in &
I realized that my words
destroyed anything we had ever been.

With the breath I have left,
I hope one day
to show you how sorry
I really am.

-Blocked-

You slip out the back door
leaving it a crack open,
hoping I wouldn't notice.
Your absence
created such a void
in my life
I am reminded every day
that you are gone,
you decided one day
you didn't want me
in your life anymore.

-Dodie Concerts & Secret Hand Shakes-

Separated by distance,
we fell apart
over time.
A pile of shattered pieces
on the floor,
we became nothing more
than hard memories
we try to forget.

-I Should've Know We'd All Become Stranger-

I was a sunchild
as you were of the moon,
such beautiful opposites
that often work
in a wonderful harmony.
Your soul longed for the sea,
letting it's peace
fill your heart.
Mine found solace
climbing mountains
letting the heat of day
revive my soul.
We were never meant
to be the same,
the sun & moon
do not compete for the spotlight,
they simply compliment each other
in the roles they're meant to play.

-Lost in Envy-

Maybe this wasn't how our story ends,
maybe we were supposed to grow
so much more than we did.
Maybe we met at the wrong time
in our lives.
Maybe, just maybe,
God will bring you back to me
when we become the people
we were meant to be.

-Maybe I Don't Know How Else To Let You Go-

Anxiety takes a hold
on my heart.
Why am I scared to see you?
It's not like we haven't
done this before.
We've had fights &
we've argued,
only to always work things out,
yet, somehow I know this time's different.
I feel like I'm being forced to meet
this new person,
a stranger,
one I'm not sure I'll like
or who will like me in return.
More than you,
I'm worried about me.
I'm worried I'm not over
all the emotions that were triggered in me.
What if I snap?
Or worse,
what if I become so cold
I shatter like Ice,
pushing you away forever.

-January 4th 2018-

Memories of my past
are seen in everyday light.
There were some good times
we had together,
now every time I walk outside
I see a little bit of you
In everyone I meet.

-Your Essence is in The Crowds-

Once you look up
to see the people in your world,
those ones that you love most,
that is when you gain
everything you can lose;
but, it's also
where our adventure begins.

-Conversation, Part one-

You tell me
"We have nothing to lose."
You say,
"There's a world to see,"
but you cut
everyone out of the picture &
often ignore
that "we"
means more than just yourself.
I know it's hard to see
you have people who love you,
more than anything
you just have to look up & realize
I'll always be there for you.

-Response, Part Two-

Let's go on an adventure, darling,
there's so much of this world
we haven't seen.
There's so much to lose
yet so much to see,
it'll be worth it
if you take my hand &
come with me.

-Proposition, Part Three-

There once lived a girl & her Monster,
they had been the best of friends.
The girl aspired to be so many things,
she poured herself into everything
with such passion;
The monster latched onto anything it could
destroying things in its path
believing the worst in itself &
everyone else.
No matter how much it had done though,
the girl still believed the best &
loved it dearly,
she could see the best in even the darkest creatures
she knew all the wonderful things
the monster could be.
The Monster had let her believe in all the possibilities
but it had become so comfortable in what it was,
deep down,
it didn't want to change.
To become something new,
something good,
was an all-terrifying thought.

There would come a day
where the Monster's darkness
would break even her &
she would walk away
carrying all the hurt

given to her over the years.
Losing her invoked the greatest change
there ever could be;
Shattering the stone around it's heart,
the Monster was no longer
void of emotion,
it no longer fed into pain
for the pain it had caused itself
was too much to pass to another.
Though the girl & the Monster
went separate ways,
they both found a way to live
happily ever after.

-I Was The Monster, This is My Story-

She was caring
beyond all belief,
her words
sweeter than honey.
She had a love so deep,
it made her strong.
Her love was like the ocean &
she never knew
she was drowning me.

-I Took Her For Granted-

I thought I had moved on,
I thought it had finally stopped hurting;
Yet, as I stand here
at the finish line of my goal,
I reach for my phone
only to let it go again.
I had come a long way
but you were still my first call,
my only call,
even after everything that had happened.
There's a stabbing pain
in my chest
as I tear open old wounds again,
the pain still as fresh
as day one.

-It's The Same as Picking at Scabs Until They Bleed-

The sting of losing someone
it never really goes away,
you just have to live with it
co-existing with memories
that invade your mind
through everyday life.
We move forward
as best as we can,
trying to make up for their absence,
but the void
that death leaves behind
isn't one that can be filled.

-I'll Never be Ready to Tell You Goodbye-

Her wavy hair flowed wild in the wind;
Covered in daisy chains &
henna tattoos
her soul was free,
untamable by the world.
She was fully herself &
one of the kindest souls
I had ever met.
With music in her heart &
light reflecting in her hazel eyes,
she changed the world
with just one smile.

-She Was The Moon-

You said that you loved me too much
to ever walk away,
that's when I realized
that we loved differently;
Because I loved you enough
to know that walking away
was the best
for both of us.

-We Were a Part of Fate-

A rush of infatuation
as sparks fly
the moment
your lips met mine.
Our hearts long
to call it love
but we knew this wasn't it.
This feeling fades
over time,
love stays
knowing fully
the faults you carry
but not wanting a life
that doesn't have you in it.
Love is more than a fleeting moment,
more than electricity
between two bodies.
Love doesn't break your heart like this,
lust does.

-We Were Distractions-

I confused comfortability
for happiness &
being relied on heavily
for fate.
I hadn't been happy
for a long time,
I didn't leave
because I didn't know
what happiness looked like.
I told myself that this
was as good as it gets,
if only I knew then
what I know now.

-Being With You Never Felt Like Home-

Perhaps, we did not want a love
to distract or
help us run away.
All we really wanted
was a love to heal us &
show us that the strength
inside our souls
is enough to face the world.

-Bandage Me Up & Help Me Stand-

We were always competing.
Always trying
to do one better.
"Friendship,"
that's what we called it
but we were too young &
too broken
to really know
what friendship looked like.
Maybe we'll meet once again
when we've found healing
on both sides.
Until then, I'm wishing you
a better life,
a better love,
& friends that shine brighter
than the stars,
complimenting your night sky.

-Sun and Moon-

Though we don't talk anymore,
I find that my mind
wanders to the thought of you sometimes.
We grew apart
into separate lives.
No matter the things between us
I hope you are well,
I hope you found happiness too.
All I ever wanted for you
was to see you reach a place
you felt you belong.

-Tear Stained Piano Keys-

I've made mistakes
in this life of mine
but taking time loving you
wasn't one of them.
Perhaps my only regret
was ever letting you go.

-Should I Have Chased You?-

On my darkest days
I am so overwhelmed
by those I have lost &
things I could have done
that I feel alone in everything.
I'm starting to wonder
what it would be like
to miss someone
without the feeling
destroying my soul.

-I'm Not Allowed Such Luxury-

We are not broken
in unfixable ways,
we are shattered pieces
falling into place.
Everything that breaks us
is bringing us one step closer
to becoming truly whole.

-Art in Progress-

The world is like this snow globe
I hold in my hand.
I watch in excitement
as events unfold,
the people in this town
living lives of their own
so picture-perfectly captured.
Accomplishing,
loving,
helping,
finding happiness
while synthetic snow flutters
around them.
I watch with longing
I'm so close yet so far away,
I am separate from this world.
Out of place,
different,
broken,
I'm only on the outside
looking in
not able to take part
in those things around me.
I see those lives right in front of me
unable to make connections,
I reach out but they're too far away
just on the other side
of this glass between us.

125

I understand their stories,
they haven't seen mine.
What if this glass is shatterproof?

-How I See My Autism-

I crossed worlds
in search of myself
traveling around this strange land.
I look for God's hand
in the sunrises & sunsets,
hoping He'd write His plans for me
across the sky & as plain as day.
I knew I was meant to be here,
to run from my past,
to find closure,
to pick up broken pieces &
figure out what I have left.

Something new.

I find it in the streets
walking to the center of this town,
spotting a reflection.
is that me?
I ask the face I no longer recognize in the mirror.
Confidence bleeds out in her smile,
she nods.

It took me months to find this moment,
to heal these wounds,
to become assertive in who I am, &
to rise above the opinions
of those around me.

The girl I've become looks ahead,
unafraid of what the future may hold
because she knows we still have a purpose
yet to be fulfilled.

-Horizons Anew-

We all have our stories
of how things happen,
of how we view ourselves
but what if the world isn't that simple?

Everyone has their perspective,
who was really the bad guy?
The Dragon, the Knight, or the Princess?
We had all done
what was right in our own eyes,
we pointed fingers &
cursed the name of someone else.

The moment I overheard you
describing yourself using the same words
I held in my heart too,
I questioned what was real anymore.
Was I as heroic as I once thought?
Were you the bad guy
I always painted you out to be?
What if none of us were monsters,
just victims with broken minds
hitting each others' triggers just right.

Perhaps stories always have a deeper understanding
that go beyond what our minds decide,
what our eyes may see,
what our hearts may feel.

-No One Tells The Same Exact Story-

We give parts of our lives,
permanent things we cannot get back,
too temporary people
silently begging them to stay
to love us for who we are.
What if we stopped
listening to society
when they tell us that this is how it should be?
What if we start saying no?
What if we took ourselves back &
pursue a life worth living,
finding people who accept you
for who you are, not what you can do,
helping you grow into who you're meant to be.
Who we are &
everything we have to give
is far too valuable
to be wasted on a life
that you can't call your own.

-What if We…?-

May we learn
to speak in search of understanding
& listen
with intent to learn.
My hope is to breathe
the kind of love
this world needs more of.

-Growth-

We write
to understand ourselves.
We read to know
that we are not alone.
Ink-stained pages
are my comfort.
The words I write,
the pages I read
are where I find light
on even the darkest days.

-Take Me to Where I Belong-

Though there is an end
to every beginning,
it needn't be done
through heartache & tears.
You must remember
that the end can be a beautiful thing,
for even the sunsets
can be more beautiful
than sunrises.

-Find The Beauty Where You Are-

Sometimes we find words
that speak to our souls.
They tell us who we are inside &
remind us to never give up.
I captured all these things
I held in my heart &
had them pressed on a page
to look back on
when things get hard.

-The Binding of Spilled Ink-

The grass beneath me,
the sun starting to rise above me.
I long for more days like this,
to search along trails &
find all the places I've never seen before.
The birds seem to call out to me
singing of their adventures,
making my heart
wish it could fly.
Maybe I was a free spirit
after all.

-Summer Nights-

The air feels soft
against my face,
as if someone I love
caressed it in their hand.
Summer nights skies
colored in deep blue,
fireflies come & go
all around me.
A feeling
touches my heart &
I know without a doubt,
this is where I belong.

-Summer, Part 2-

Spending my whole life
hiding behind weakness & insecurity,
I let my happiness sit
on the other side
of an answer I may never get.
Hoping I could wish away my illness
the way one would
take power away from
Rumpelstiltskin,
with only its name.
The world doesn't work
like all the storybooks,
with the answer came more pain.
More questions,
more doctors,
more treatment…
Less
    control
           on
                my
                    side.
I wish I had learned
that happiness isn't having
all the answers
but finding joy
through all the pain &
taking time to go
dancing in the rain.

-I'm no Mistress Miller-

I've spent so much time
looking for myself
instead of living life &
letting who I am find me.
So let's get lost
in what we don't know &
enjoy the adventure
life throws our way.

-404 Not Found-

I found you here.
Maybe I found
a little bit of myself too.
You showed me
that soulmates
aren't always lovers,
they can be friends too.
Maybe that's what I needed
all along.

-More Than What I Made You to Be-

Stay close to me,
hold my hand &
never let it go.
As I walk through
my darkest hours,
I just need a friend.
Anyone.
To stay & remind me
that I'm not going
through this alone.

-Hello Darkness-

I am often asked
why I find so much joy
in rainy days &
sadder things;
It's because happy
can be too bright sometimes &
there's a deep beauty
in sadness
that this society has yet
to understand.
A beauty I see,
a beauty I understand;
It's like a little secret
that I share
with the world around us.

-Sally Sparrow-

Water crashing all around us.
We were on top of the world &,
in that moment,
I felt I was going to be okay
for the first time
in a long while.

-Rainbow Falls, 2018-

I thrive on the innocence
of a new relationship,
I wish it would last
longer than it always does.
I'm addicted to effort,
the flirting,
light kisses,
& affirmations we share.
I long for the willingness
of spontaneous adventures,
inconvenience is only minor for us.
I start losing myself
when you try to rush me,
light touches aren't enough
when you try to pull me into
something more intimate.
Maybe it's fear
or the longing for some lasting connection,
but I always felt in my heart
that love was never something to rush.
If it's meant to happen,
it'll happen naturally
or not at all.

-You Can Call Me Demisexual-

I was once told
that I say 'I love you'
too many times.
That I've somehow
forgotten its meaning
or how to use it.
I think I've done just the opposite.
I love fully,
with every fiber of my being.
Love bubbles over from my heart &
to hold in that kind of weight
may just kill me.
I say 'I love you'
because I know what it's like
to rarely hear those words.
I know how it feels
to not be allowed
to say them either.
I say 'I love you'
too many times &
I mean it from the depth of my heart
every single time.

-I Am Full of Love to Give-

Perhaps love isn't as easy
as we want it to be.
We keep thinking we're doing it wrong
when we don't fit
this cookie-cutter mold
for a relationship.
What if we were honest?
Love is complicated,
it's messy.
It's an argument
followed by understanding & apologies;
It isn't falling for a perfect person,
it's choosing them
even after you know them for their imperfections.
It's speaking two separate languages &
learning to communicate together.
Love is compromising even when it's hard,
never going to bed angry
though fighting makes you tired.
Love is asking God daily
to teach you wisdom & understanding,
taking your partner for the good times &
the bad,
because you never want to spend
a day without them.

-You, My Love, Are Worth It-

Life can be
a lonely dance,
if we live every day
without a splash of romance.
Not every spark
is meant to be more,
to take all that dark
you hide in your soul.
Yet, when love is true,
it will be there
when your days are blue;
Lonely nights to be shared
to remind you
that you are not alone.

-Every Time, Every Season-

Caught up in flattery,
I have to take a step back.
You deserve so much more
than to be another rebound
in my life.
I value you more
than I fear the hurt
I'm still running from.
When you do fall in love
I want it to be the real thing for you,
not just a passing distraction for me.

-More Than a Fleeting Moment-

I lost myself so many times
in years past
that I couldn't really tell you
about the girl in the mirror.
All I know is she's growing,
she's learning,
a healer
yearning to reach out &
touch the lives of those around her.
She may not have all the answers
but that's okay too.

-I'll Find Her Someday-

The world started making sense again &
the cloud of confusion
that so often blocked my path
faded away the moment I chose myself.
I decided that I was worth too much
to waste my energy playing this game.
I am worthy of time & love.
This is the moment
I choose to stop giving different parts of my life
to those who do not want me back.

-Self Care-

Music, to me,
is an escape from this very world
every stroke of key,
every note sung,
every story has the possibility
to take you on an amazing journey
teaching you wonderful things.
A musician is simply
a storyteller
spinning songs in the open air.

-My Hideaway-

There's more than one way
to explore the world.
I walk through pages
covered in words that shape stories,
visiting worlds that make me
never want to come back
to this harsh reality.
Look for me & I won't be here,
I'll be searching for who I am &
a place that I belong.

-Wanderlust-

I'm the kind of person
who falls halfway in love
with almost every person I meet,
because you can find something
to love in every person
if you take time & look hard enough.
Every connection I make
becomes a colored string
tying their heart to mine &,
no matter the distance between us
or the years going by,
my heart will always
remember your name.

-A Form of Synesthesia-

It's not about the past
you leave behind,
but what you do
with days ahead.
Every breath you breathe
is a gift
that not everyone will have today.
Don't take your days
for granted.

-Move Forward With Gratitude-

You asked me how
I could've ever moved on
from you.
My answer is simple, darling,
I moved on
because you gave me
no other choice
when you left.
I pressed forward
because that was all
there was left to do.

-Accepting The Hand You Dealt Me-

Healing isn't an exact science to study
but I've learned a thing or two
of what not to do.
One of life's greatest teachers
is making the wrong choice &
learning from consequences
that remind us not to make
the same mistake twice.

-I Don't Know Much, But This Much I Do-

You asked if I was better yet,
only days after a fight.
It's taking me months,
even years,
to find that answer;
With a weak smile,
long after you're gone,
I answer to myself:
Not yet, but I'm getting there.

-What if I Had Said Yes?-

Perhaps the world
was not meant to understand
a soul like mine,
it's a mystery God has written
in the sky.
I find myself on the most starry nights,
maybe you'd see me too
if you lay down beside me
under this night sky.

-Maybe I Was Made This Way-

Space,
I'm still learning
that I shouldn't always feel guilty
leaving messages on read
or not opening them at all.
Sometimes a pit still forms
in my stomach &
I ignore my need for space,
assuming I'm the only one.
I'm still figuring out
that sometimes people need
a break from me too.
Maybe someday
I'll turn off my phone,
log off my computer,
& be at rest
without worrying
that I'm letting the world down.

-Words & Their Meanings, Part One-

Patience.
It is a word
that doesn't make much sense to me.
Why should I wait
if I know what I want,
if I know what I feel right now?

Timing.
God is helping me realize
that just because something is right
doesn't mean *right now.*
A perfect moment can bring it all together
saving you from tears & heartache,
perhaps that's why patience exists too.

These two words work together
in intricate designs
that make up life.
Maybe good things really do
go to those who wait,
maybe things get better
with time,
& maybe, just maybe,
God works out every detail
in the end.

-Words & Their Meanings, Part Two-

I'm a runner,
experienced,
I've been doing it my whole life.
I run from everything:
My problems,
fears,
anxiety,
depression-
toward the great unknown &
my need for adventure
as it calls my name
in a moment's notice.
I bury myself
in all life's distractions,
maybe when I resurface
those things I didn't want to see
will have gone away for good.

-This is My 10K-

There is ink
running through my veins &
countless stories
written on the tables of my heart.

-Stories a Tattoo Needle Can Tell-

Every day
there's a war inside
between who I was &
who I want to be.

-Victory is Subjective-

Nostalgia is something often felt,
making me wonder
if my memory
is giving me pieces
of who I am
that I may put it together
like a puzzle in front of me.

-Always One Piece too Short-

I wasn't born
wild & free
I became who I am
because of what Christ
did for me.
I've danced with joy
on my best days,
I've felt comfort as I cried
in my darkest hours.
A traveling soul &
a longing to see
the deepest parts of nature,
I have a thirst for adventure
that will never be quenched.
I've seen God paint hope
in every sunrise &
a calming peace
in the way the sunsets,
it still overwhelms my heart.

-Be Still My Soul-

I paint worlds inside my head,
letting my imagination run as wild
as it chooses.
I find stories in everything I see,
I write songs in the air,
& I find poetry written in the way
your eyes sparkle
as you speak of something you love.
My mind is a complicated work,
I can do so much
but I find it hard to remember
the word "hello".

-Hello Sweetie-

I had always been told
I was a child of the night
rising with the moon.
I find my peace during the day
on my adventures with you
through every touch of nature.
Everyone was wrong about me,
I was a sunchild
meant to rise in the morning
with the beautiful colors
of the sky.

-To Touch The Mountains or Reach The Sky-

The truth I was so afraid to admit,
this identity is made of glass
ready to shatter
on the floors,
when I finally say out loud
the words I had buried deep inside.
I don't remember.
It was soft whisper
at first,
it grew until I stopped shaking.
No longer bound
to the girl who died that day,
I don't feel the need
to fill her shoes &
follow her path.
God has given me my own path,
I spent so much time
trying to be the girl
so many missed that I forgot
to look for my purpose,
my power,
the way I will shake the earth &
leave it changed in ways
unforgettable.

-Glass Ghosts-

There's an adventure
inside my soul.
There's a longing
to find myself
along the paths I travel.
I know where I must go,
I know where my heart
longs to be.
There at the center
of where the spirit leads me
is where I'll find
the rest of who I am.

-Life's Grand Adventure-

I was told, long ago,
that with a wish
follows a great curse.
I was naive to think my story
was exempt in any way.
I asked to leave a mark on the world
not caring how I left it behind,
if only I listened to the warnings
of those around me
on the path I would choose to wander.
They're all gone now,
I destroyed every last one of them.
All that I touch
fades to ruin.
My words are an avalanche,
tumbling downwards &
destroying all that's in its path.
This will forever be my curse.

-Midas Had His Gold-

I follow the roads ahead,
not caring about the things around me.
I find you here,
in the middle of this route
I made with such detail,
you weren't a part of the plan.
Your name wasn't doodled
here on my map,
yet,
there you are in front of me.
Your heart was broken in two &
so was mind,
healing found us at
such an odd time.
You never promised to stay,
only that adventures weren't meant
to be done alone.
I no longer care about the roads ahead of me,
so long as wherever I am in the end
I still have you.

-Follow Me Down These Broken Roads-

I had found love
in the spring,
one I thought
could never be taken away.
It faded as the sun grew hot
& you walked away.

Summer is running,
a breath of fresh air
as the wind blows through my hair
& my favorite song
plays on the radio.
I never want to stop,
I'll never go back,
I'll never slow down again.

But I did,
as autumn found me
bringing a season of self-discovery.
The leaves started to fall
& I found a new beauty
in this world.

I had always dreaded
the loneliness of winter
& the bitter cold
that comes along side the snow,

though as I found myself in fall,
I found peace & solitude this winter.
maybe the seasons have a purpose after all.

**-My Four Seasons, A Cycle of Motivation
Mixed With Depression-**

To feel your hand
brush against mine,
an accidental touch.

You meet my gaze,
holding it for what seems
like forever in a short time,
a momentary blush.

Arms wrapped around me
in a hug that lasts
a few seconds too long,
I never want to let go.

A thought of you here,
a smile toward you there-
I stumble & fall
deeply into the thoughts
I hide inside my head.

Completely rational,
I walk down the road &
into love with you;
Having questioned practical outcomes
knowing very well I'd be willing
to spend the rest of my life

being your friend
with the possibility
that you'll never love me back.

-Tanglewood Lights-

5AM conversations don't just happen,
they're made when effort
bleeds out on both sides.
Promises of going to bed soon
but we both know it's not true.
We don't want the conversation to end,
we don't want to walk away,
wishing 'good nights' could be whispered
mere inches apart
in the same bed.
You'd never say it
but maybe
you were a little in love with me too.

-Your Words Were Wrapped in Blue Spring-

Love is a scary thing,
it makes the whole world
seem alright again,
problems don't seem so big
with someone there to solve them with you.
Everything seems so perfect
that it terrifies you.
What happens if it ends?
Nothing good exists for too long,
especially not in my life,
everything has a painful end.
I hope you stick around,
I can already tell
if you leave
yours would hurt the most.

-Please Stay With Me-

I am falling
deeper in love,
every moment I spend
with you.
I just hope
you figure things out &
catch me in your arms
before I hit the ground.

-Less Than Lovers, More Than Friends-

Is it too soon
to ask you to run away with me?
Is it too soon
to plan for every part of forever?
I don't care about the details,
we can do anything
as long as I have you.
Let's just drive
with no destination in mind,
an alternative CD playing &
windows rolled down.
Let's just go where no one knows our names.
It's too early to say 'I love you'
but you're the only love
that I ever want;
So, instead,
I'll ask about your day &
make sure you get home safe
in hopes of getting the message across.

-I knew You Were My Forever-

You are the light
in a darkened sky.
You are the guide
to help me
find my way back home.
Home.
It was a fairy tale
inside my head
until you came along.
You are the hope
I hold so dear
next to my heart.
You are the love
I never knew I could feel.
You became all the things
I never knew I was missing,
all the things
I never knew I needed.
I started living
the moment I met you.

-You Brought Out The Best in Me-

My perfect date
is deep conversation
on a walk in the woods.
It's holding your hand &
showing you how I see the world.
It's the stories I get to hear &
everything you let me learn about you.

My perfect date
is 2AM dances in the kitchen
while I make hot coco
on the stove.
It's getting so lost
in the music that isn't playing,
we forget about the world.

My perfect date
is helping you around the house
while we sing loud music off-key.
It's a light kiss here,
a smile there.
To know you're letting me
be a part of your world.

My perfect date
is being held close
under the stars.

It's contemplating the universe &
God's plan in it all.
To be with you,
the one I love most.

My perfect date…
                    … Is you.

**-More Than Sitting on Opposite Sides of The Same
Room-**

When I am no longer
shiny & new,
I hope you still say
I love you
& mean it with your whole heart.
I hope that
we grow old together
never old of each other,
to know that you were with me
to the end.
That you were truly happy
& that's why you stayed.

-Partners in Crime-

I ran my fingers
across your scars,
the marks that life
has left on your body.
You were embarrassed
to let me see them
because the world has taught you
that they would make me
love you less.
I smiled.
You never looked more handsome.
I love you.
Every part,
every scar,
they are a part of your story &
so am I.

-Don't Be Afraid to Show Your Scars-

To be in love
is a beautiful thing.
To love someone
who loves you back?
Now that's magic
not everyone will experience,
so hold it tight.

-This Side of Forever-

Poetry is written
in the way we breathe
this very air together.
My words can spill out
In the way my fingers
glide gently across your skin.

-Love is a Language-

One moment
in your arms
has the power to stop time &
become part of forever.
Every moment I can hold onto
is worth the space
you left in between.

-Six Hundred & Seventy Four Miles-

In the lobby of your heart
where you so kindly let me in,
I saw pictures of us.
Memories hung on the walls,
moments that we fell so deeply into
forgetting to pull out a camera.
A tiny sign placed beside the door,
"Don't touch, fragile artwork,"
but perhaps
it didn't speak of
the pictures on the wall.
Your very heart was a masterpiece
to hold in awe &
you trusted me not to break it.

-When You Opened Your Heart So I Could See-

We didn't share many firsts
but with every touch of my soul &
moment spent,
you became my favorite.

The best good morning kiss
when I'm rushing out the door
on a Monday.

The most gentle hands
that hold me,
when my sickness gets too much
for me to handle alone.

The sweetest smile
when you tell me you love me
every day
as if it were the first time.

The most genuine words,
dipped in sugar,
to remind me I am worthy
when my demons tell me otherwise.

You,
my love,
are my greatest gift.

-All The Ways To Say I Love You-

I want to know
the secrets your heart
doesn't yet know how to share.
I want to hear
all the words
you're scared to breathe &
their importance to you.
To see the parts of you
that you say aren't worth time;
To be the one who figures out
who you are,
in trying to show you
how important you are to me.
You are so much more
than what the world
is pushing you to be.

-Inspired by Dodie-

My mind is a garden of roses
made of glass,
both fragile & full of beauty.

A garden like mine
is watered
with words of kindness
& blossoms
with moments of healing.

I've created a safe place
I know I can thrive in
while feeling loved.

We often mistake
acts of soft kindness
for weakness &
fragile beauty
for vanity.
What you see
as my weakness
is my strength;
kindness is not
the presence of innocence
nor is inner beauty

source of vanity,
holding both is empowerment.

To mess with a glass rose
is a dangerous game.

Shatter me & I will cut you.

-Glass Roses-

"Yet I Will Myself to Grow"
By Kyle Medlin

Call me old fashioned
Maker of flower crowns and honeysuckle
This earth I make my own

Call me fertilizer on asphalt
Call this foolish?
Yet
I will reclaim this ground.
The earth is in the business of reclaiming
So I trumpet the song I have
A song of stained face
 and scraped knees
You say
      Scathed
      Battered
      Burned
I say
      The Waiting
      The Encore
      The Reprise

Do not forget
I am still a Rose -

Surviving so many Winters.
and Yes,
This lovely
        Worn
            Continuing
            Did surprise me too.

Acknowledgments:

Dakota-I don't know where I'd be without you in my life. You are my better half in every way. Thank you for supporting me & never giving up on me.

Brenda-Girl, you are amazing & worth so much more than you realize. You have always accepted & loved me with no questions asked, I couldn't ask for more.

Meg-You are one of my constants. No matter my stage in life, our paths always cross & you have been a voice of reason or a listening ear.

Bricia-Some of the best people are the most unexpected in your life. You are my biggest cheerleader & spontaneous friend, I finally get to live all these random adventures because of you.

Kennedy-You are one of the most amazing people I know, so kind & so hard working. I'm insanely happy to call you my friend. Photoshoots & silly adventures are what life's made of.

Tat & Kait-You two were some of the first people I've met that allowed me to be myself without judgment & you helped me

196

up on bad days. You showed me that who I am is amazing no matter who disagrees.
Sam- You are so beautiful, inside & out. Thank you for checking on me even in the busyness of life. You are a better friend than you give yourself credit for. You are going to do amazing things.

Sincerely,

A N E

Instagram: a_n_e_poetry
TikTok: anewritingservices

Kyle's Instagram: itskmeds

www.ingramcontent.com/pod-product-compliance
Lightning Source LLC
Chambersburg PA
CBHW060510130626
46553CB00002B/449